DATE DUE

JUN 28 1996		

DATE DUE

DISCARD

PRINTED IN U.S.A.

Phone: 815-692-3231
Fax: 815-692-3503

2×4yrs

COLYPSO
Cousteau

LITTLE SIMON

Simon & Schuster Building, Rockefeller Center

1230 Avenue of the Americas, New York, New York 10020

Copyright © 1991 by Hachette, France and The Cousteau Society, Inc. English translation copyright © 1993 by The Cousteau Society, Inc. First U.S. edition 1993. All rights reserved including the right of reproduction in whole or in part in any form. Originally published in France by Hachette Jeunesse as *LOUTRES*. LITTLE SIMON and colophon are trademarks of Simon & Schuster.

Manufactured in Singapore   10   9   8   7   6   5   4   3   2   1

CREDITS

The Cousteau Society, Jacques-Yves Cousteau, Jean-Michel Cousteau

Author: Pamela Stacey, Christine Causse. Photo Editor: Judy K. Brody

Translation: Jeannine C. Morgan. Project Director: Lesley D. High

With special thanks to: André Demaison, Thierry Piantanida,

Veronique Platt, François Sarano.

Photographers: Jeff Foott, Richard Bucich, Frank S. Balthis,

The Cousteau Society, Kennan Ward.

Library of Congress Cataloging-in-Publication Data

Loutres. English, Otters / the Cousteau Society.   p.   cm.   Summary: Examines the physical characteristics, behavior, and feeding habits of the sea otter.

1. Otters—Juvenile literature.   [1. Sea otter.   2. Otters.]   I. Cousteau Society.   II. Title.

QL737.C25L6713   1993   599.74'447—dc20   92-34177   CIP

ISBN 0-671-86567-6

The Cousteau Society

OTTERS

LITTLE SIMON

Published by Simon & Schuster

New York   London   Toronto   Sydney   Tokyo   Singapore

SEA OTTERS

Weight and size
Baby: 4–5 lbs., 20 inches
Adult: 66 lbs., 70 inches with tail

Life span
20 years

Food
Sea urchins, shellfish and crustaceans

Reproduction
Marine mammal
8–9 months gestation

Lives on west coast of North America
from California to Alaska

Can dive up to 180 feet depth

The otter is one of the very rare animals that uses tools.
It breaks open its food with a stone.

A protected species

The sea otter spends its whole life in the water.
Its webbed paws make swimming easy.

The otter is a small mammal. Its thick fur protects
it from the cold, like a warm winter coat.

The otter wakes up after sleeping all night curled up in the seaweed.

Safe in its seaweed bed, the otter will not drift away and get lost in the currents.

It's time to wash up. Scrubbing and rubbing, the otter licks itself clean.

An otter bath takes time. Clean, thick fur is needed to keep it warm.

After its bath, the otter rolls over and floats on its back to rest in the sunshine.

Paws up! With all four legs out of the water the otter suns itself to stay warm.

This mother otter takes good care of her baby. She carries it on her stomach.

She leaves to catch food and wraps the baby with seaweed, so she can find it later.

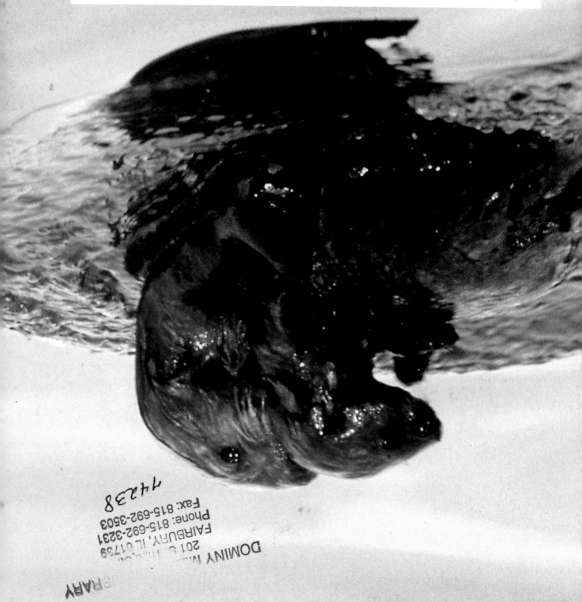

Otters eat crabs and sea urchins. They dive down deep to find food. Crunch!

Sunning, bathing, or munching a crab, the otter is at home in the sea.